DIRTY LITTLE

DOG

KATE SKYLARK & SOPHIE JENKINS

Dirty Little Dog

A horrifying story of child abuse and the little girl who couldn't tell a soul

Disclaimer

This book is based on true events.

The names of people and places have been changed to protect the innocent.

Cover photograph is posed by a model and is used for illustrative purposes only

For every book sold, a donation will be made to the NSPCC

CONTENTS

PROLOGUE

Mother was not a cruel woman; indeed, there was not an ounce of intentional harm in her. But I would sadly go on to harbour immense resentment toward her because of what was to happen that summer. My mother didn't beat us, she didn't put us down, shout and swear, or drink too much and forget to feed us. She didn't bring unsuitable men home or gamble away the family allowance. No, my mother's fault was simply to be absent-minded to the point of neglect. She was a clever woman in many ways, but her lack of common sense and a seeming inability to think clearly and foresee the possible or even likely consequences of a particular course of action would lead to catastrophe.

Mum, I know you did not mean for what happened to happen. I know you would have taken a different action if you could have foreseen what was to befall me that summer. But, Mum, any normal mother, any normal *person* should have been able to sense the danger, and so prevented the terrible harm that would come to such a vulnerable and unworldly child. I want to forgive you, Mum. But I can't, not yet. Perhaps writing this story will do it. Perhaps I will feel the cathartic effect of 'getting it all down on paper' and in doing so will find the place in my heart where forgiveness lies.

If it's 'out there' then it really happened. In some sense I feel disbelieved, not because anyone has ostensibly told me so, but because I have never had that experience of telling my story. I have never had anyone tell me 'it wasn't your fault', 'you were just a child'. Maybe I should have told teachers, policemen and therapists. But that's not my way. I didn't want to be identified forevermore by crimes that were committed against me. There is no comfort in that. But there *is* some sense of comfort to be found in telling *you*, my readers. By telling you, and by being believed, I feel less alone with my story. You may never see my face, and I will never see yours, but I thank you in advance for any kind or sympathetic feelings you may have toward me. With the safety of anonymity comes a lack of inhibition. I am free to tell my story as it happened, without fear of judgement or looks of disbelief.

So here it is: my story.

CHAPTER ONE

It was a hot summer in 1976. I was a confident, precocious yet naïve eight-year-old, intelligent but unworldly. I grew up in what looked outwardly like the idyllic country village, chocolate box-like with its thatched cottages, central pond, horticultural shows, fetes, country fairs and festivals. My mother had married my father young, spending the next ten years producing five large, healthy babies with surprising regularity. He then left her to raise his large brood alone while he went on to start a new family in South Africa. We scarcely missed him. My two sisters, two brothers and I were brought up well enough, with little money but far from anything approaching poverty. We squabbled a lot but it was never serious. We also played together a great deal and enjoyed a large, bustling house overrun with pets of all sorts. Cats, dogs, hamsters and gerbils were our childhood companions. As children growing up in the country, we had no gangs, no places to 'hang out', no youth clubs, shopping malls or community centres. Pets, reading, one small TV and the immense Dorset countryside filled our summer holidays.

For children such as us, the country events – the fairs and fetes – were an exciting spectacle, a day of excitement where we could gamble our pennies on ferret races, and steal sips from our parents' squashy plastic glasses filled with beer or cider.

It was late summer, almost time for us to return to school after the long break. I was particularly looking forward to a county show that was to take place on the final weekend of the holiday. My granny, as payment for my spending a whole day helping to weed her garden, had paid me a wage of two pounds. This was a huge sum to a child in 1976, and I had already a vague plan of how I would spend it on the coming Saturday at the county show. I had worked out a little rule in my head for the spending of money at these sorts of events: I would spend some on food while I was there, some on playing games or entertainment at the event, and I would spend some on 'something to take home'. This had actually been my granny's rule and I had simply copied it. I liked the rule. It made me feel like nothing had been missed out. Two whole pounds would mean I would have plenty to spend on each type of attraction. Probably, I would start with an ice cream or lolly, lots and lots of turns at picking straws or playing cards to win prizes, and enough left to find an interesting souvenir on one of the bric-a-brac stalls.

After lunch on that Saturday, my mother bundled all five children into the Triumph Dolomite – four in the back and my eldest sister, as always, in the front. At the grand age of eleven, only she was allowed this privilege. She was also the only one to wear a seatbelt. This is not because Mum didn't enforce a seatbelt rule in the back of the car, but simply because there weren't any. In 1976 most cars, ours included, weren't even fitted with rear seatbelts.

The car never started first time. My mother always had to 'choke it' – something that I always thought sounded horrible. I imagined she was strangling the car to make it behave, and the rattling, scraping noises it made while she pumped the accelerator only reinforced this image.

It was a loud and argumentative trip to the horticultural show. We were always a loud family, never demure or particularly refined. I remember this trip well because my older sister was not too pleased about the fact that I had a whole two pounds to spend whereas she and my other siblings had only 50p. My mother had given this gift to all four other children. I didn't receive the 50p from my mother because of the two pounds given to me by my grandmother. So if anyone had a right to feel hard done by, it should have been me.

'I can't afford to be giving you 50p, too, Sophie, when you already have so much money,' Mum had said.

Well, that didn't make any sense to me at all, and it was just grossly unfair in my eyes. It's funny how children have an absolute and clear notion of fairness and justice, and adults will often overrule that fairness with illogical and irrational reasons such as 'I can't afford it'. If Granny hadn't given me the money, then my mother would have afforded giving me the 50p. So why was it different now? As I said previously, I was precocious but naïve.

The village of Newton was about ten miles away along narrow country roads. Often, my mother would have to pull in to the side of the road and wait to let another car pass. Inevitably would come the wave of acknowledgment and thanks as the other car passed. When, very occasionally, the wave of thanks didn't come, my mother's judgement was brutal. She would gasp with shock at the rudeness of the other driver, shout '*Excuse ME!*' and denounce them as 'clearly not from 'round here'. It seemed to me that not waving thanks for a driving courtesy must have been one of the worst crimes in the world.

We arrived at the site and parked up in the designated 'car park' – just a lumpy and cowpat-filled field with all the animals removed. We all tumbled laughing out of the car, the earlier squabbles now forgotten in our excitement to get to the show. My mother paid our admission fees and we entered. I clearly remember the feeling of excitement, of expectation, like a large wonderland had opened up before me. It was all unknown, all just bubbling, rumbling potential.

It blows my mind to think he was already planning his attack, while I walked in, happy and oblivious. *He* was already there; somewhere he was standing, walking, talking, plotting. I think back to that moment repeatedly. Why was it *me* he took? Of all the children at that festival, why did I walk into harm's way at that moment? Many times over the years I have wished that another child had been taken in my place. As an adult my feelings have matured, but as a child I spent many nights wishing some other little girl had gone through it rather than me.

CHAPTER TWO

For the first hour, we walked around as a family, a traipsing shoal of blonde hair and wellington boots. My mother was on the lookout for her sister, who had arranged to meet us with her own two children - my cousins and playmates, Matthew and James. We children were already scanning for things we could do, things we could *have*. Constant calls of 'Mum, can I have…' rang out.

Eventually, Mum caught sight of Auntie Jean and my cousins. After hellos were finished, the two women set off in search of a drink, leaving us children to wander around unsupervised. This was the norm back in 1976. My oldest cousin, Matthew, was fourteen, and was considered more than capable of looking after six younger children. We ran and played and laughed at his showing-off antics. We thought him the funniest and most entertaining person ever. He swore and made a trick with his hands that looked like he was pulling his thumb off. At the age of fourteen, he seemed like a fully-grown man to us younger girls.

We bought lollies from an ice cream van, always an orangey one for me, always a choc-ice for my sister.

It was some time after buying ice creams that I accidentally-on-purpose got separated from the group. I really wasn't sorry to be apart from my family by this point. I always relished the opportunity to be away on my own, doing my own thing, and I was keen to spend the rest of my money. On my own, I wouldn't be subjected to ridicule or disdain from the others over my choice of souvenir – 'You don't want to buy *that!*' I could imagine my older sister saying, 'That's so babyish!' The same went for the games I liked to play. I loved to 'waste' my money on the sorts of games where you picked a card, or a duck, or spun a tombola to have the chance of winning a prize. My sister thought these totally wasteful, and she would not hesitate in telling me so. Perhaps she was right. Perhaps I should have listened to her because it was wasting money on one of these very sorts of games that led me to danger.

I drifted slowly past the food stands and hook-a-duck games, eventually stopping at one stall. This one was covered with cuddly toys. There were plenty of the 'throw three darts and win a cuddly toy' type stalls. But they hadn't interested me. Most of the toys on those stalls were really very poor quality with flimsy material and weak stitching, and sometimes the seams were just glued together. But the stall that had caught my attention was quite different: this stall had superb plush toys of all sizes and different types of animals. There were large teddies as the 'main' prizes but also dogs, owls, cats and tiny mice. All of them were expensive and realistic and quite different from the poorly replicated Disney characters on the other lesser stalls. In 2014, when I wrote this book, realistic stuffed toys were commonplace. But back in 1976, soft toys were still usually made to look cartoonish, with garish fluffy fur, orange plastic eyes and oversized heads. The toys on display at this stall were like nothing I had ever seen before. They looked like real animals. I was dumbstruck. A soft brown and white dog with floppy ears entranced me. He looked almost like he could have been a real live puppy with his soft silky coat and brown glass eyes. If I could win that dog, I thought, I wouldn't even need to spend money on a souvenir to take home.

I didn't see the man standing behind the stall until he spoke. He was sitting on a chair and had been hidden by the toys.

'Five tickets for 10p,' I heard a voice as I saw the owner of the stall rise to his feet.

I don't remember having a particular impression of him at this point. I just remember he was tall and very thin. Five tickets for ten pence seemed an absolute bargain to me. With five whole tickets I would be sure to win the dog, so I thought in my childlike mind.

'Okay,' I smiled and handed over a ten-pence piece.

The man placed a large container in front of my face. It was a big plastic Tupperware tub and seemed filled with sawdust. I looked up at him, confused as to what to do.

'There you go, my love. Just pick out your five tickets and make sure they're good 'uns.'

I looked again at the barrel of sawdust and realised that it was actually filled with little pieces of folded paper. They were raffle tickets folded over, over, and over again until they were quite tiny. I could see from corresponding raffle tickets stuck to the toys that it was only numbers ending in 50 or 100 that were winners. There were two 'big teddies' which each had the numbers 500 and 1000. The middle-sized animals like dogs and cats and owls had tickets that were multiples of 100. My dog was number 600. All the little mice sat on tickets ending in 50.

As I looked into the tub, I felt I could sense the winning tickets, and as I drew out five little paper bundles I was absolutely sure one of them would win me that dog. But as I unfurled the little scraps of coloured paper I was dismayed that not one of the five tickets had that same number.

'Never mind, love. Have another go,' the stall owner said, shaking the tub of numbers invitingly in front of my face again.

'No, thanks,' I said shyly, stepping back from the stall and walking away.

I continued to wander around the other stalls, looking for something to catch my eye. But I wasn't happy. I *wanted* that dog, desperately. This was the sort of ferocious longing only a child could have. That dog was beautiful. It was not like any other fluffy toy I owned. That was a dog that would be given a name, brushed and cared for. I wondered if my mother would buy it for me and I briefly considered going to look for her to ask. But I knew what the answer would be: *If I have to buy you a dog, I'll have to buy everyone a dog. And I'm living on the breadline.* This was one of her favourite sayings but I never knew what it meant at all. I always imagined my mother trying to balance on the sharp edge of a bread knife, teetering and tottering about as she tried to walk along the knife edge. But I knew it had something to do with not having much money because she would bring up the 'breadline' comment whenever we asked for something. I grew up imagining that my mother had less money to survive than almost anyone in the world. No, asking her was simply not going to work.

There was only one way. I would just have to go back to the stall and buy another five tickets.

CHAPTER THREE

Immediately, I felt brighter, and with a fresh feeling of hope and surety that this time I would be successful, I returned to the fantastical cuddly toy stand. I could see it from a way off, with its coloured animals, beckoning, an irresistible lure for all small children. By the time I reached it again, its magnetism had drawn a fair crowd of little children. Seeing so many other kids, I panicked that one of them might win my dog before I had a chance to have my go. I watched as each child had his or her turn and sighed with relief as each walked away disappointed. As the little crowd dispersed, I found myself alone in front of the magical stand once again.

'You back again, love?' the man smiled at me. I saw he had yellow-stained stick-like teeth. With hindsight, he was probably only in his early thirties but to me he looked like an old man. I imagined he was probably around fifty. He was very ugly, I thought, with a thin drawn face, sunken cheeks and those nasty teeth.

'Can I have another go, please?' I asked.

'Right you are,' he said jovially as he took my money and handed me the tub of tickets. I carefully took out another five. But to my utter dismay, that second set of tickets did not contain one winner, not even a mouse ticket. By now, I was hooked on the idea of winning that dog. Little children are quite capable of being bitten by the gambling bug, if only in this tiny way. So I handed over another ten pence and took another five tickets. *Nothing again!* I was crestfallen, not least because I knew I had now spent so much of my money.

'Bad luck, eh?' the man said, looking at my distraught face. My overpowering longing allowed me to forget my shyness, just for a moment, and I said in a loud voice 'I just *really want that dog!*'

'Yeah, I really like that one, too. I've got a dog who looks a bit like him at home.'

'What's he called?' I asked with newfound confidence. I liked to talk about pets. 'I love dogs.'

'He's called Barney. I've had him since he was a puppy.' And pointing to the cuddly dog, he added, 'He looks like Barney when he was little.

Do you have a dog?'

'We used to,' I replied. 'His name was Rusty. But he died. He had to go to the vet's and the vet gave him an injection. But he still died.'

I was enjoying talking to this stranger. He didn't ask me the usual sorts of stupid questions that adults ask like 'How's school?' and 'What do you want to be when you grow up?' He asked me loads of things about myself, about all my pets, their names and what they liked to do. He asked me what my dad did and I told him he was away in South Africa and that we never see him. I told him about the money that had been given to me by Granny, and the way I was intending to spend it. He was very interested in everything I had to say and, even though he was very ugly, I thought he was one of the nicest men in the world. He told me he was a teacher, so I knew he wasn't a bad man.

As children we were all told not to talk to strangers. All children know they must run and tell a teacher or a policeman if a stranger offers money or a lift in his car. But no one ever tells children that sometimes people *tell lies about being teachers or policemen*. To a child of eight, when a man tells you he is a teacher, this places him in the category of completely trustworthy people. The moment you hear he is a teacher, he instantly becomes as safe as your mum or dad.

'Look,' he said suddenly. 'Would you be able to help me with something?'

'What do you want me to do?' I was intrigued.

'I need to take a break and go and do some things. But I can't leave the stall. Would you be able to watch it for me and make sure no one steals any of the teddies? I'll pay you a pound if you do it properly and make sure nothing gets nicked.'

How could I possibly have refused a request like this? Since reading about other victims of abuse, I now know that this is a ploy that abusers will often use. When a child is asked to help a grown-up they will often feel a kind of honour has been bestowed on them. Being asked to help makes them feel special, and so find it almost impossible to refuse. And I was no different.

'Okay, I will,' I said with great seriousness.

'What's your name?' he asked.

'Sophie Jenkins. What's your name?'

'My name's Martin. And if your mum comes by, just tell her I'll be back at three.'

And so I had my first proper paid job. And, boy, was I proud. I guarded those toys like my life depended on it, watching every person who walked by, looking for signs of criminality. I felt immensely important as I, a wistful looking little blonde girl, stood behind a stall full of teddies. I even let some people pay for tickets and have a go at winning prizes. This situation would never happen now. Parents don't leave children unattended, babysitters must produce references, and eight-year-olds don't preside over market stalls. But things were just *different* then. And while it may have been a little unusual to see an eight-year-old in charge of a stall at a county fair, it certainly didn't look abnormal.

As it was, Martin didn't stay away for very long, and I was actually a little disappointed to see him walking back towards me, far earlier than I expected.

'So, what's going on here then? Did any burglars come for them teddies?' he joked. I proudly told him that not one toy had been stolen.

'Well done,' he said. 'You must have been a very good stall-helper. That's definitely worth a pound.' He then produced a green pound note and passed it to me. I was thrilled.

But by now I was enjoying myself too much to walk back into the fair. I didn't want to leave my new position as 'stall-helper'.

'I can stay and help you for a bit longer if you want,' I offered, hopefully.

'Well, that *would* be a good help. It gets tiring working on this stall all day. But what I need is a really *good* helper. I have another job that needs doing but it is really special. I need some more tickets folded up but it needs to be done properly. I think perhaps you are a bit too young to do that.'

'No, no, I can do that!' I assured him.

And so, for another couple of hours, this man, Martin, became my friend, talking about me, encouraging me, complimenting me on my cleverness and on how grown-up I was. He laughed a lot at things I said, and I showed off more to make him laugh even more with his gravelly smoker's voice. He also paid me another two whole pounds for my afternoon's work.

Martin told me he liked to do a lot of these sorts of country fairs and festivals, travelling around and staying overnight on campsites, sleeping in a tent. I thought that the most exciting idea in the world. I decided that was what I would like to do when I was a bit older. Martin also told me that the money he raised was for charity – the RSPCA.

For a small girl who was lacking a father in her life, Martin seemed the most wonderful man possible. What I didn't like about him was that he had a permanent cigarette in his fingers that he sucked on deeply before blowing the smoke out of his nose. I was both fascinated and horrified by this. My family took a very dim view of smoking in general, and certainly blowing smoke out of your nose was very common. Martin had yellow fingers that I found very confusing. At that age I didn't know that nicotine could permanently stain skin. He also stank of cigarettes, a deep, rank, sour smell nothing like fresh smoke, but an old and dirty stench.

'It's a shame you can't help me tomorrow, too. But I'm going away to another festival a long way from here. I could really have used your help, and I would have given you that dog, too.'

'I'll come with you!' I offered excitedly.

'No, you can't,' he shook his head. 'I have to leave in a minute and drive quite a long way away, and your mum will want you home soon.'

'No, she won't mind,' I assured him.

'Well, you'll have to go and ask her and bring her here for me to talk to.

But you'll have to be really quick because I'm packing up soon.'

So off I raced, looking this way and that for sight of my mum.

CHAPTER FOUR

It didn't take too long to find her, easily recognisable with her long black hair and flowery skirt down to the ground. It was now gone five o'clock and by this time she had caught up with the other children. It appeared that Auntie Jean and my cousins had already left and my family were ready to go home.

'Mum, mum!' I gasped. 'I helped a man on his stall and he wants me to help again tomorrow and you have to come with me and talk to him. *Right now!*'

'What are you talking about, Sophie? What man?'

'The RSPCA man. He needs me to help him. But you have to say it's allowed. But he's leaving soon. *Please, Mum!*'

'Sophie, we need to go. I don't know. Where is this man? We don't have time...' Mum said in an irritated voice. The younger children were getting fractious and she just wanted to get home.

As fate would have it, we had to pass by Martin's stall on the way to the exit. As we neared it, I could see he hadn't left yet. In fact, he hadn't even begun to pack up. On seeing me, Martin strode towards us with a charming smile and offered Mum his outstretched hand.

'Ah, you must be Sophie's big sister. I'm Martin Bloom. Delighted to meet you. Is your mum around?'

I grinned widely. My mum got these sorts of comments a lot. She was very pretty and looked much younger than her years. I knew she loved it when people thought she was my sister.

'Silly!' Mum smiled back at Martin. 'I'm her mother, and these are my children.'

'Oh my goodness! I would never have thought... I'm sorry. Mrs...Jenkins. Sophie has been a fantastic help to me this afternoon. I do hope you don't mind that I let her help me on my stall.

It's quite difficult running the stall completely on my own.'

They chatted away. Mum was completely charmed. She was particularly impressed to hear that Martin was raising money for the RSPCA. Mum had actively worked to raise money for this charity herself and it was dear to her heart, she told Martin. They got on so well that I seemed to have been forgotten while they nattered on about all sorts of grown-up subjects that I couldn't understand. Mum laughed a lot, throwing her head back in an overly demonstrative way, and Martin smiled back, showing his matchstick yellow teeth. I felt a little annoyed. Martin was supposed to be *my* friend, not hers!

'Mu-um!' I whined, pulling at her hand. 'Can I go with him tomorrow? *Please, Mum?*'

'What's all this about tomorrow?' she said distractedly.

'Well, I told Sophie I'd have to clear it with you,' said Martin, serious for a moment. 'It's not a big deal but I could really use Sophie's help tomorrow at a big show I'm going to in Kingston. It's really just to help me prepare the tickets, and to look after the stall if I need to nip out and get some lunch or go for a pee.

Usually I have someone to help, but I'm on my own this weekend.'

'But where are you going to be staying?' asked Mum.

'I always take my tent and I've already booked a place at a campsite outside of town. I have a couple of sleeping bags and pillows in the car already because I usually bring my own daughter, Justine, to help.' And he then added, 'She's with her mother this weekend.'

Mum nodded, understandingly. She knew what it was to be a single mother.

Martin went on, 'I have a Primus stove for making tea in the morning, and I have some bread and jam for breakfast. We always have loads of fun,' he smiled. 'The only thing is, I need to leave really soon, in a few minutes in fact. Would you mind if Sophie came with me? If you let me know your address, I can bring her back by tomorrow evening.'

This is the bit I don't understand. I run this over and over in my mind, and even now I can't really make sense of my mother's reaction. Perhaps you are a mother. If so, you probably live in some fear of your child being abducted by a stranger. Even if you don't have children, you will know that every child is taught not to talk to strangers. If a stranger offers you gifts, refuse and run away. Every mother strives to keep her child safe and away from danger. And here was an odd-looking single man, someone my mother had just met, offering to take her eight-year-old daughter away *for the night.* Planning to stay *in a tent.* But rather than pull her children close, and walk hurriedly away, or even tell the police, my mum just said, 'I can't see why not.'

You couldn't see why *not?* How could you not see all the countless reasons why not? How could you not sense even a hint of danger? Mum, he was a complete stranger. He apparently needed an eight-year-old to work for him. He wanted to take me away from you in a car to stay overnight *in a tent!* And to top it off... he had a stall full of cuddly toys! He might as well have said he was taking me to see some puppies.

But without a hint of hesitation, my mother agreed to let her eight-year-old daughter spend the night in a tent with a complete stranger. She even made my brothers and sisters help Martin to the car with all his toys and equipment, smiled as I got into the front seat of his car and waved as we drove

CHAPTER FIVE

I was happy and excited as we drove away from the festival. We hadn't even had to stop and pick up any of my things from home. Martin had promised my mum he would buy me a toothbrush on the way to the campsite. He had some of his daughter's pyjamas in the car and I was to wear the same clothes tomorrow. I was sitting up front in the passenger's front seat, not in the back like a little child. And Martin didn't even tell me to put my seatbelt on! Mum would never have allowed that to happen, and it made me feel immensely grown-up and naughty, not to be wearing a seatbelt. Martin smoked almost constantly, holding the cigarette between his nicotine-stained fingers. He was oddly silent compared to his earlier chattiness. In fact, he hardly spoke at all. I talked occasionally but mostly he just ignored me, as if his mind were on something else. We drove for perhaps an hour before Martin turned into a narrow country lane, bumping his way down what seemed like more of a dirt track than a road. Eventually, he turned into a large field that I took to be the campsite. He drove across the field to the far hedge and turned off the engine. It was getting dark now and must have been about eight o'clock, but I could see well enough to tell that ours was the only vehicle in the field.

'Where are all the other people?' I asked, expecting to have seen a mass of caravans and tents.

'It's not that sort of campsite,' replied Martin. 'I just know the farmer here and he lets me use his field to stay in. You stay in the car while I put up the tent.'

He had become so different since we left the festival. He wasn't being jolly and laughing at my jokes any more and he didn't ask me any more questions. In fact, he was not even looking at me most of the time.

A few hours earlier I had been laughing and smiling in a summer festival, with sights and colours and children everywhere. Now I was sitting in a cold and silent car in a pitch-black field in the middle of nowhere. For the first (but not the last) time that weekend, I began to regret going with him and longed for home. It seemed ages before the car door opened.

'It's ready,' he said. 'I've got the kettle on.'

The idea of boiling a kettle in a tent seemed quite exciting to me and I brightened, keen to see this stove and how it worked.

Martin opened the flap of the tent and I peered inside. I was pleasantly surprised to see that he had laid out two sleeping bags, pillows, and all the things for tea. There was a kettle making a rumbling noise on top of a stove, a tiny table laid out with cups and plates, a bottle of milk and a plate of sausage rolls. There was also an unopened packet of fruit shortcake biscuits. The whole tent was lit up with several camping lanterns, and best of all, all the fluffy toys were arranged at the back of the tent, as if waiting for a teddy bears' tea party. Martin pulled across the two pillows for us to sit on, and we sat and waited for the kettle to boil.

'So, Sophie. Do you have a boyfriend?' Martin asked suddenly. This didn't seem odd to me. Adults will often ask this question of little children and I was glad he was being friendly again.

'No,' I replied. 'I used to have a boyfriend when I was little but I don't have one now.'

'What was his name?'

'Mark Cartwright. He goes to my school.'

'Did you ever kiss Mark?' asked Martin, and then he added, 'Did he ever show you his willy?'

'No!' I said, embarrassed.

'Would you like to see a willy?'

I didn't reply. I just rolled my eyes at him. Inside, I was squirming with embarrassment. I had got to the age where the sight of a couple kissing on the TV while my mum was in the room was enough to send me into a fit of excruciating shyness. Adults could be so rude sometimes, I thought.

The kettle was now boiled and I was glad that the conversation had to stop for a bit. He made tea in the mugs and added milk and sugar. The tea was too strong for me, but I drank it anyway. I ate two sausage rolls and plenty of biscuits, dipping them into my tea until they softened. I was now feeling happy again. The tent was quite warm from the stove and it felt cosy with all the animals watching us drink our tea. Martin brought out a pack of cards and we played snap. We played I-Spy and a memory game.

I went to the shops and I bought a pink gorilla.

I went to the shops and I bought a pink gorilla and some chocolate biscuits.

I went to the shops and I bought a pink gorilla and some chocolate biscuits and a fire engine.

I went to the shops and I bought a pink gorilla and some chocolate biscuits and a fire engine and….

We were staying up late and I was having fun. All children love to stay up late, and the fact that we were in a tent made it doubly fun. It must have gone midnight when Martin eventually said it was time for bed.

And so the nightmare began.

CHAPTER SIX

He turned off the stove and was rinsing the cups with a bottle of water when I suddenly remembered something.

'We didn't get me a toothbrush!' I exclaimed.

'It doesn't matter, we'll get one in the morning,' assured Martin. 'I don't brush my teeth every night anyway.' I was shocked. My family were very strict about tooth brushing, and I remember thinking that if he had brushed his teeth every night, perhaps they wouldn't have been so yellow.

'Where are the pyjamas?' I asked.

'It's too hot for pyjamas tonight. You'll get really warm in that sleeping bag anyway,' he assured me.

I started to get into my sleeping bag. The zip was undone all the way down and the top half was just folded on top of the bottom half.

'You'd better take your jeans off, or you'll get all sweaty in the sleeping bag,' Martin suggested. 'And don't zip up the sleeping bag because if you need a wee in the night, you won't be able to get out.' I didn't like this. I remember it didn't feel right somehow, although I really didn't know why. I don't think I believed that wearing jeans would make me sweaty and I certainly didn't think it would be difficult to open the zip if I needed to later. But I did what he told me.

I lay down and closed my eyes while Martin undressed. I opened my eyes just for a second to see his skinny white body, his long bony legs folding like an insect as he got into his sleeping bag. He was wearing nothing but a pair of pale blue Y-fronts. I closed my eyes again and tried to sleep.

It was only a few minutes before Martin started to make noises like he was already asleep. No one could fall asleep that fast, I thought. It always took me ages to fall asleep. Martin rolled over to face my back and a hand fell on my side, as if he had absent-mindedly done it in his sleep. I inched away but as I did, he made a snuffly sleeping noise and snuggled up further so that his body was tight against mine. His left hand moved onto my bare tummy. My heart pounded. I was just massively confused. Was he really asleep? It seemed like he was doing this intentionally. I tried to pull away again but each time I did, it seemed to stir him into snuffling noises and more supposed sleepy movements. Each time this happened he moved closer and tighter against me so that eventually his bare chest was against my back and his legs were touching mine. His sleeping bag was also unzipped, but the open edge of his sleeping bag was next to the open edge of mine, allowing him easily to get closer. I really began to feel uncomfortable. I didn't like having a grown man cuddled up behind me and I hoped he would eventually turn over to face the other way.

I lay still, not budging an inch. I couldn't risk moving and prompting him to another of his 'snuggling-up' movements. Then the tea hit my bladder.

'I need a wee,' I announced, getting up suddenly.

'Okay,' he answered instantly. He hadn't been asleep at all.

I began searching for my clothes.

'What are you doing?' he asked.

'Putting my jeans on,' I could hardly go out into the cold half-naked. He seemed convinced and I put my jeans back on. They were now freezing cold and felt damp to the touch.

'I'll take you,' he offered.

'No, I want to go on my own,' I assured him.

I walked out alone into the dark field, looking around for a place to go. The grass was dewy and my feet were bare. There was no bush or suitable hiding place but the grass was quite long in places. I had walked a reasonable distance before deciding to squat. Before I did I looked back to the tent to see Martin, with his head out of the flap of the tent, watching me. What was he doing? Why did he want to watch me going for a wee? Why had he gone so weird? There was no chance that I was going to go to the toilet in front of him. Strange though it sounds, I decided to just squat down and pretend to pee. It was more acceptable to my eight-year-old mind to make him think I was urinating. I couldn't have let him actually watch me go. *That* was unthinkable. I pulled up my jeans and headed back to the tent, my bladder still full.

'You need to take your jeans off,' Martin said as I clambered back into my sleeping bag, fully clothed.

'I'm freezing cold,' I said and turned my back on him again. I felt safer now with my trousers back on. The thick denim was cold and damp from the long grass and was now icy cold, but I felt more protected from his body and its horribly close proximity. My feeling of safety was short-lived. Martin didn't even pretend to be asleep this time but simply sidled up behind me, and immediately started to slide his hand down my tummy, groping his way inside the elastic of my pants.

I said not a word. My mind was hot with confusion and my tummy was full of snakes. I needed him to stop. I needed him to stop this, *now!* I felt his finger poking and probing around lower and lower, and with that, I found my voice.

'I don't like it!' I blurted out.

'Don't worry. It's all going to be okay. I'm not going to hurt you.'

'I still don't like it! I want to go home,' I trembled on the point of tears.

'You're not just a little girl, are you?' he said disdainfully. 'I thought you were more mature than that.' And then he added, 'This is just what people do who like each other. You do like me, don't you?'

So that was it. He fancied me. He wanted me to be his girlfriend. I must have made him think I wanted him to be my boyfriend, too. If this was just 'what people do' then I had to accept that. And so I just lay there as he undressed me completely, turning on the light so that he could see what he was doing.

I don't remember seeing his penis. I don't remember any pain at the time. In later years I liked to think this was because he had only a very small penis. It may also have been that he didn't manage to penetrate me fully. I do remember him climbing over me, trying to push something against me between my legs. I remember turning my head to the side to escape his foul breath as he grunted and made a noise like he was enjoying food - *Mmmmm...mmmmm.*

I had no fear that I would die. I never thought he would kill me or injure me. I genuinely thought he wanted me to be his girlfriend and that this was just what grown-ups did. I hated it. My revulsion at his breath was so bad I thought I was going to vomit. He utterly disgusted me. But I didn't know this was *wrong*.

The thought that Martin was a bad man who was committing a crime didn't even enter my mind.

He couldn't help it. He fancied me. I just wished I had never met him.

I turned my head to the right to escape his breath, and my eyes fell upon the brown and white dog. It looked so friendly and cute and I reached out to it. I grabbed it with two fingers and brought it to cuddle to my chest, sinking my face into its plush fur. A little friend, a sanctuary in the middle of this hell I was going through. I crushed him against my face, as if I could block out the reality behind his softness.

'Yeah, that's it, Baby. Hold the dog, cuddle him,' said Martin as he suddenly got up and, still kneeling between my legs, started to move his hand up and down between his legs. All the while his eyes were on me, an eight-year-old child, desperately trying to find solace in a cuddly toy. After a little while his face changed. His face went red, and he looked like he was going to explode or shout at me. I was then shocked to feel a bit of warm liquid splash against the skin of my bare tummy. I was appalled. How could an adult do something so disgusting? I thought he had urinated on me. Only years later did I realise it was something different.

Once he had ejaculated, Martin said not another word. He got off me, got into his sleeping bag, *zipped it up*, and went off to sleep. This time, I knew he was genuinely asleep because he snored loudly. Martin hadn't even given me anything to clean myself up with but instead left me alone with a puddle of his filthy mess to deal with myself.

In the months and years that followed, it would be this failure to help me clean myself off that would infuriate me the most. It is this detail that still makes my blood boil and invokes the greatest feelings of hatred toward him.

All he had to do was hand me some tissue or a bit of kitchen roll. Martin had both rolls of loo paper and kitchen roll packed in the bags that contained the tea things. But rather than get either for me, he just lay down and went to sleep, leaving me to have to grope around for something with which to wipe myself. The lantern was still on and I could see my own coat lying close to me. I knew a tissue was in the pocket, as it always was, and after retrieving it, I did my best to wipe this vile 'wee' from my skin, throwing the tissue out of sight to the back of the tent.

I still had my dog for comfort although his fur had also become wet with Martin's fluids. I wiped the filthy liquid off against the groundsheet as best I could and cuddled him tight. He was a little damp but he was still my friend. I buried my face into the dry part of his fur and breathed his clean new-toy smell

CHAPTER SEVEN

This was the first night ever that I would spend the entire night without sleep. I was frozen cold to my marrow and desperate to pee, but I dared not move a muscle for fear of waking him. I did not sleep for one single second. Years later I would go on to develop a severe and chronic sleeping problem. While undergoing various treatments for this, therapists would often ask, 'When was your first memory of missing sleep?' and my mind would shoot back to that terrible freezing night in the tent. But I would never, ever tell any of them of that night. Perhaps I was in denial but I just wasn't willing to allow that Martin was still having an effect on my life.

Hour after hour passed. I couldn't sleep a wink. I lay wide-awake, too cold to be comfortable, too appalled to sleep. I also had not emptied my bladder and it was now painfully full. I was becoming desperate to urinate but there was not a chance that I would move and risk waking my tormentor. I can't tell you the thoughts I had. I think when a mind that is so young experiences something so horrible it cannot make any thoughts at all. I just wasn't capable of taking it all in. I only remember a sort of confusion. And I remember tears streaming down either side of my face as I tried not to sniff too loudly, lest I wake the monster that snored next to me. At that point I felt neither shame nor fear. I just felt utter confusion and some relief that my abuser was truly asleep.

The dawn came early and I remember the tent becoming very gradually light. It was probably the first time in my life that I had ever noticed dawn breaking. With the comforting light of dawn, my mind seemed to clear and I felt braver. I thought to the day ahead – the Sunday festival where I would be helping him on the stall. It no longer seemed an exciting adventure. I actually felt horror at the thought that I would have to be in his company all day. And what if he wanted to do 'that' again? Not for the first time that weekend, I felt I was actually going to be sick. I had to use a trick I had learned when much younger after seeing a cat hit by a car. I just forced my mind to think of something nice, like a birthday or Christmas, until the feeling of sickness passed. That helped.

This was the first time since meeting Martin that my thoughts turned to escape. In the hours that passed between dawn and Martin waking up, I had time to think and plan my escape. If I could get my clothes on without waking him, I could maybe sneak out of the tent. But I couldn't walk along the roads, I realised, because he might drive past and see me.

So on that cold dawn, my mind was whirring trying to think of another way of escaping my abuser. I came up with what I thought was a perfect plan. I would wait until Martin woke up, and then tell him he had to take me home because I had just remembered I had something on today that I had to get back for. That was it. That was my brainwave, my perfect idea for escape. I don't think I even thought up a specific reason, such as having to visit my granny, or a forgotten party. I was so sure that this would do it, that this would convince

Martin to take me straight home, that I felt lifted and hopeful. I actually began to look forward to him waking up so that I could get back home all the sooner.

Martin stirred and I heard him mumble, 'You still here?' It must have crossed his mind that I would try to escape.

'Yes. I'm here. And I've just remembered something. I have to go home,' I blurted out. 'I have to do something today that I forgot about.' And I breathed a sigh of relief. I had said it. Now he would *have* to take me home.

'No. Your mum said I was to have you back tonight. I'll take you home tonight.'

My heart sank and I started to cry. This couldn't be happening. I had been convinced my ordeal was over and I was about to get away from him. Now I had a whole day with him to cope with once again. But it was about to get worse.

'I'll make some tea in a minute,' he said with his gravelly smoker's voice. The tent was filling with his rank morning breath, sour and strong. 'But I want you to do something first. I'm going to show you something. I want you to warm me up a bit.'

He reached inside my sleeping bag and grabbed my right hand, balled into a fist. He pulled it toward his crotch.

'Open it. Open your hand!'

I obeyed and he pressed my hand against something warm and hard, like a long bone. 'Put your hand around it. Hold it. Like this. A bit tighter. That's it. Now move your hand up and down, slowly. That's it. That's it.'

He held his hand around mine as he used my small hand to pleasure himself. After a short time he made that same angry noise like he was exploding, and let my hand go free.

What was next? Was this 'game' going to continue all day? Would he try and push his penis against me again? The sick feeling returned and I started to retch. I tried to think of Christmas thoughts but it wasn't working this time. I was crying silently. Tears were falling but I was making no sound.

'Do want some tea?' Martin asked as he dressed himself. 'I'll get the stove on and warm us up.'

I shook my head. Martin ignored me and made two cups of strong tea again. He also made me a jam sandwich. I couldn't eat a thing.

I couldn't drink a thing. I would have vomited if I had tried. My bladder was now bursting with pain and my mind was in turmoil. I needed to urinate *desperately* but I dared not go in front of him. I would eventually have to wet myself and that thought was horrible to me. I remember thinking, '*This is the worst thing that's ever happened. This is the worst thing that's ever happened...*' I just clutched my dog and wiped my tears away with my fingers.

'Hey! I didn't say you could have that dog yet!' Martin snatched my little talisman from my hands and threw it back with the rest of the toys. 'You can have that once you've finished helping me today.'

He packed up while I sat silently in the car.

CHAPTER EIGHT

We drove immediately to a public toilet in what seemed to be a small village. The toilets were housed in a grey stone building that stood apart from all the others. At the sight of the 'ladies' sign, my bladder seemed to spring into life and it was all I could do to keep myself from wetting the car seat. But Martin wanted to use the loo himself and he locked me in the car while he went first. He only let me out to use the toilet once he himself had finished his morning business. It seemed ages before he returned and let me out of the car. The public toilet was icy cold and dirty with stone floors and broken seats. But I didn't care, because at last I was able to relieve my painful, bursting bladder.

Perhaps I was slightly in shock - certainly I was suffering from sleep deprivation - but I don't actually remember much about that day's events. There are only flashes here and there of random things, odd events.

I remember entering the festival and Martin telling me, 'Get rid of that sour face! You'll get me in trouble. No one will buy any tickets from you looking like that!'

I remember him chatting amiably with parents as they bought tickets and failed to win prizes. 'Is this your daughter?' they would ask. 'No, this is Sophie. She's my friend's child. She's helping me out today, aren't you, Sophie?' He was so charming with other people. But he had almost given up talking to me. Gone was the friendly dad-like man of yesterday. It its place was just this gruff-voiced ogre and his stinky yellow fingers.

I remember being left alone a lot to mind the stall while he was off doing things, enjoying himself, grooming other children perhaps...I really don't know. I must have looked a strange sight, a forlorn and bedraggled eight-year-old girl, unsmiling and miserable, in charge of a stall full of teddies. Despite my glum face there were a lot of customers. Perhaps they felt sorry for me.

I remember no one winning any prizes and people asking 'if I had remembered to add the winners' to the barrel of tickets. I remember being horribly embarrassed at this, as if it was somehow my fault. I also became ravenously hungry at some point, and I remember Martin bringing me a polystyrene cup of 'great soup' as he described it. It was actually just gloopy orange cup-a-soup type sludge, sweet and tasting of plastic. But I think I drank it.

I don't remember packing up. I don't remember anything until we were sitting in the car in the car park, ready to leave. Martin once again made me masturbate him before we left. He forced me to sit with my legs spread apart while his left hand was forced down the front of my pants, his rough yellow fingers poking around, trying to probe a way inside me. My little hand was on his horrible organ and his right hand was on mine, moving up and down as he made that horrible noise: *Mmmmm…mmmmmm*.

I never once looked at what I was doing between his legs. Something just prevented me from doing that, as if by seeing his penis everything would become even more real. I just stared past him through the window, watching people just a few feet away getting into cars and driving away. I could hear their voices. But I didn't call to them. There was not a chance of that. In fact, I was terrified one of them would see what we were doing.

CHAPTER NINE

I have a brief memory of driving home. I now had my dog, which I gripped tightly as I nodded in and out of sleep. I remember Martin dropping me off at the end of my road, some way from my home.

He did not come in and speak to my mother. I don't remember him thanking me. I don't remember him saying goodbye, just something like 'there you go' as he opened the door and let me out. I remember hearing the car drive away. It was an orange Volkswagen Beetle and it made a completely different sound from my mother's car. You may never have noticed, but almost all Volkswagens used to have a very distinct sort of ticking sound to their engines. The newer cars must have different engines, but sometimes I still hear a car with that distinctive tick-tick-tick-tick-tick-tick-tick sound. Even today I can't hear that sound without my blood rushing and my heart pounding.

I slipped into the house without being noticed. I remember going straight to my room and lying on the bouncy softness of my bed. *It's over, it's over, it's finished, I'm home.*

So what did my mother say? What did she do? Did she cry and wring her hands? Did she pull me close and tell me she would never let it happen again? Did she call the police to get him arrested while the evidence was still fresh? No, she didn't do any of these things. She didn't say anything at all, because I never told her. She was busy with the other children and hardly seemed to notice that I had come home. She didn't even ask me much about my night away or the day I had spent at the festival. She eventually made some humiliating comment about my new toy dog like 'isn't that a bit babyish?'

I think what isn't always appreciated is that it is not always fear that stops a child telling its parents it has been abused. Sometimes, children are simply too *embarrassed* to tell. To my mind, the thought of telling my mother the details of what had just happened was *excruciating*. We were not a family that talked openly of such things. If even a relatively tame sex scene appeared on the television while the whole family were watching, my mother would get up and switch channels. Even if a couple starting kissing passionately in a film, my mother would pick up a newspaper or magazine and pretend to start reading it. Isn't it ridiculous? I didn't tell my mother because I was too *embarrassed* to do so. When I think back, I feel so sorry for my eight-year-old self at this point, trying to make sense of things, in desperate need of help but being prevented from asking for it by sheer fear of embarrassment.

It is this that breaks my heart most about child abuse and all the stories I have heard from other people: little children, experiencing the most awful terrors but not able to tell a soul. I know at this very point in time there are children, right now, maybe you pass them in the street, who are hiding terrifying secrets.

To my mind, we must work not only on keeping our children safe, but on teaching them what to do when faced with danger. We tell children to avoid strangers but we don't tell them why. For a long time, I thought strangers snatched children because they had none of their own. I thought they 'stole' other people's children so that they could raise them themselves. Child sexual abuse is so taboo, so appalling to our adult ears that we would rather not mention it in front of the children. But in doing so we leave these children completely unequipped to deal with danger when it unfortunately *does* arise. If I had ever had children, I would have taught them about sex almost as soon as they could understand. I would have taught them about danger and encouraged them to speak to me about *everything.* Nothing would be shocking or taboo. The sexualisation of children is disgusting, I agree. But I think letting them grow up ignorant of danger is nothing short of a crime.

It might surprise you that I kept the dog. A gift from a monster may seem an odd thing for a child to want to keep. But you see, the dog had been my safety blanket. He had been the one safe, friendly thing I had during the ordeal. It's not that he had kept me safe, that wasn't it. It was that he had been there with me, he had gone through it too. He had come through it with me and escaped with me. I would protect him, as he had once protected me in his tiny, ineffectual way.

And what I didn't know at the time was that this little fluffy dog, that had offered me little defence against danger, would eventually help me to defeat the monster that had once terrorised me.

CHAPTER TEN

That night and for a few days after the night in the tent I felt nothing but relief. I even felt happy that everything was back to normal. It took a few days before I knew that something was still wrong. I stopped being able to sleep properly, often lying awake for full nights. And then the bad dreams began. I would find myself naked in front of people. They weren't pointing or laughing but were turning away in embarrassment and disgust at my nakedness. I would be running around looking for a toilet, desperately trying to not wet myself. Eventually, in the dream, I would find a toilet, close the door, sit down and let my muscles go with relief as I released the urine and emptied my bladder. I would then wake almost immediately and every time I would find that I had emptied my bladder in reality, too, and was lying in wet sheets. Eight years old and I began wetting the bed like a baby. Years later, the bed-wetting stopped but the horrible naked dreams continued. Even now I will occasionally have this dream when under stress.

Everything in my life changed from that point on. I changed. Everything about my life seemed to fall to bits slowly, gradually from that day. I think back to before the event, and I can just remember life without *That* in my mind. The memory became like a constant companion. But it was not a friend; *That* was more like a bully, a captor, a constant supervisor nagging at me. I could be thinking about something completely different, lost in some activity, but all the while I would be aware of this looming horror, *That* was waiting behind the thoughts, ready to pounce out and make my heart leap and the tears prickle.

My behaviour changed beyond all recognition. I became angry. I would lose my temper and say mean things to my brothers and sisters. I would call my little sister 'an ugly cow' and torment my baby brother, squeezing his fingers until he cried. My mother never suspected that something actually might be wrong. She not once asked what might have triggered this change in me. 'You're such a hard girl these days, Sophie,' she would scold, nastily.

The bed-wetting had become almost nightly. My mother became exasperated with me. '*Sophie, this has to STOP!*' she would say with her 'on the point of pretend crying' voice. I was desperate to get her attention. I didn't have a clear concept of this at the age of eight but, looking back, it was obvious that was what was going on. I remember walking home from school and planning that I would hide in my room and not speak to anyone. 'They aren't going to see much of me from now on!' I clearly remember thinking. Somehow I imagined that would make everyone sit up and listen, notice, give me the attention I was clearly craving.

I became obsessed with the idea that Martin would one day come back for me, and that my mother would tell me to go with him. I was terrified that the doorbell would ring and he would be standing there, demanding that I come away and help him at another fete or fair. It was only a matter of time, but I knew he'd come for me. For a long time, I refused to answer the door when the bell rang, annoying the rest of my family. *Sophie's the closest! She can answer it!* But I would often just run upstairs and sit in the corner of my room, my legs pulled up tight against my body.

CHAPTER ELEVEN

And then I had the brilliant idea that I would run away. I knew exactly where I was going to go. I passed by a field with a barn every day on my way to school. I had seen this sort of barn in films many times and had a clear idea of what the inside of the barn would look like. It was just a little girl's fantasy of the fairy-tale idyllic barn, complete with friendly mice and perhaps an owl living in the rafters. The floor would be strewn with golden hay and there would be a ladder up to a sort of balcony floor. This mezzanine level would also be full of soft, warm hay, and up here is where I would live. But I didn't want to go alone.

One of my best friends, Joanne, lived a few doors away. She was a couple of years older than me and went to a different school. She was terribly mature and I really looked up to her. She would be my ideal companion to run away with, I decided. One morning I called for her at her house and she came out and walked with me down her garden.

'I've got a plan,' I said. 'How'd you like to run away with me?' Her response was immediate.

'Love to!' she said very simply. I knew she would. She was always fighting with her brother and told me she hated him. I knew she would be much happier living with me in the barn.

'But we have to go today,' I insisted. This point I was very clear about. I knew that if I left it until tomorrow, it wouldn't happen. I knew it had to be today. We had to pack and go *now*.

'Okay,' she seemed convinced.

We both went back to our houses to gather as much money as we could. I took some coins from my mum's purse and everything I had in my moneybox. We walked into town to buy supplies and bought a loaf of Nimble bread, a packet of margarine, some cheese puffs and some chocolate biscuits. We returned home and went to my bedroom, sneaking past my family with our bag of supplies. We sat on my bedroom floor to take stock of what we had. Joanne assured me she could also take some mini rolls and other items from her house without anyone noticing. She would also make a big bottle of orange squash to take with us. We sat there all afternoon, planning our new life in the barn. We never once thought about what we would do if we ran out of food, got bored or cold, or whether we would go to school. All I could think of was sitting and eating our feast on the top balcony floor of that barn, and sleeping in the hay, with no family around me. I thought of how my mother would notice that I had gone, and that made me happy. The plan was that we would slip out of our houses at eight o'clock and leave.

At eight o'clock I put on my coat, picked up my carrier bag full of supplies, and went and knocked on her door. Her mother, Sue, answered the door.

'Hello, Sophie. What do you want? It's a bit late for Jo to come and play now,' she told me. That didn't worry me. I knew Joanne definitely *was* coming out that night. Joanne came to the door and Sue went back into the house.

'You ready?' I asked excitedly.

'Oh,' Joanne said aloofly. 'I'm not coming.'

'Why?' I asked, crestfallen.

'Well, I told Melissa (her sister) and she said

it was a stupid idea, and *Happy Ever After* is on.'

'*Please* come! But I can't go on my own,' I was pleading with her.

'Yes you can,' she assured me. 'I won't tell anyone else.'

She closed the door and returned to *Happy Ever After*. I returned home and went to my room and cried my eyes out. I felt utterly alone and stupid. I was afraid my mother would find my stash of food and ask what it was all about. I didn't know what to do so I ate as much of the food as I could, spreading margarine onto the bread with a ruler and swallowing it down as I sobbed, tears falling down my face. Why it didn't cross my mind to just throw it away, I really don't know. Perhaps I was worried my mum would see me. Over the next couple of days I forced myself to eat all the supplies we had bought, stuffing the wrappers in a corner of my bedroom.

CHAPTER TWELVE

I don't know when it was that my behaviour at school started to change. What I do remember is that while I still wouldn't often cheek my mother, I came to lose all fear of disobeying teachers. I discovered that when you were naughty, nothing bad really happened. The teacher might shout or tell you off or send you to the headmaster's room, but that didn't bother me one bit. Once upon a time, being told off by a teacher would have been the worst thing possible. Being really naughty was unimaginable, something the bad kids did – the ones with the smelly clothes who had rough parents from the council estate. But somewhere along the line, being naughty became the norm. I would smile at the teacher as she pointed to the door and grin at the other children as I walked out. And I would stand in the headmaster's office and scowl at him. I wasn't remotely afraid. I felt that the more I talked back and argued and sulked, the more grown-up and clever I was. He couldn't tell *me* what to do. And every time I talked back, I felt he could see this. I felt that I won the argument every time. Without fear of teachers, I did what I liked. They were no scarier than my little brother, and I ran them ragged.

I threw screwed-up paper at the teacher. I talked constantly through the lessons. I came in late from break time. At lunchtime I threw food at the dinner ladies. I would put the plugs in the sinks in the girls' toilets and set the taps running until they overflowed. If I had been a boy, perhaps my schoolmates would have found me funny. The boys always seemed to get away with more than the girls. But the other children just drew away from me. The girls would often look shocked at me. 'Ummmm! *Sophie!* You can't do that. I'm telling Miss!' girls would say in shocked whispers. The boys just told me I was stupid and pushed me out of their way as I came toward them.

But in contrast to my brash and rebellious behaviour at school, at night I still had nightmares almost every night, waking in a pool of sweat and urine.

Time and time again, my mother was brought in to speak to the teachers about my behaviour. The last time I remember this happening, I was standing in the headmaster's office while my mum and the headmaster sat in chairs. I had become used to grown-ups discussing my behaviour in front of me. I would usually just keep a scowl on my face and let them get on with it. Sometimes I would grin – something guaranteed to get a reaction out of my mother, who must have wondered where her well-behaved little girl had gone. These days, a child who suddenly has a change of behaviour, starts lashing out, having nightmares and wetting the bed would signal a clear case of abuse or trauma. But this wasn't the view taken in the 1970s. Far from it - the fault was all mine.

'Sophie, why don't you tell *us* what you think we should do about all this?' asked Mr Jackson.

He was not behind a desk, but sitting opposite my mother in a kind of forced friendly setting, probably designed to be less authoritative and to give the impression that we were all equals in this room. Yeah, right. Mr Jackson was wearing grey trousers that were a bit too short and also too tight. He sat with his legs apart in that aggressive 'look at my crotch' way that some men do. I could see a bulge between his legs. I felt a sick feeling at the back of my throat and my heart started to pound.

'Why don't you piss off!' was my reply. It was the worst thing I had ever said. I felt immensely proud of myself and wished that there had been other children there to hear it. Mr Jackson gasped. My mother put her hands up and just said, 'Oh, *Sophie!*' But I had gone too far. The consequences of my swearing were to be terrible for me.

'Mrs Jenkins, this just can't go on,' Mr Jackson was talking to my mother again. I was a naughty, troublesome child. I was disruptive and out of control. It wasn't fair on the other children. The teachers couldn't be expected to put up with this sort of behaviour. I needed severe punishment.

'I have spoken to Miss Grimm and we have agreed that Sophie should join the hut for the foreseeable future,' Mr Jackson said firmly.

The hut! The genius headmaster's answer had been to banish me to the remedial class. I don't remember the correct name for what this class was

- remedial, backward, retarded. It certainly wasn't 'special needs' as is now used. We knew it simply as 'the hut'. This was a sort of Portacabin set aside from the main school. While it was in the grounds of my school, it was actually a sort of catch-all for the waifs and strays of three schools. It was filled with disruptive and disturbed children, but also it catered for those poor kids who had no emotional problems, but who were just slow learners, perhaps slightly deaf or dyslexic.

'No!' I suddenly became terribly afraid. 'Mum, no! Please don't let me go there!' I started to cry and reached to grab her hand. 'Mum, please! I'll be good, I'll be good! I promise!'

'It's too late for that, Sophie,' said Mr Jackson.

'It won't be for long, love,' said my mum, unpicking my fingers from hers. 'It's just for a while, to give us all a break.'

Even now, I still can get a sense of the horror I felt in the headmaster's room that day. It was a feeling of complete panic, of being utterly alone, of having no one left to turn to. I felt a huge urge to run out of the door and away but I had no where to go, no one to go to.

I had been one of the best-behaved and brightest children. I had been able to read long before I even went to school. My handwriting was beautiful and I had always been the one chosen to write the 'Get well', 'Congratulations on your new baby' or 'Sorry you're leaving' cards for teachers. It was fair to say I was probably a bit of a teacher's pet. After eight years of perfect behaviour, my brief period of unruliness was rewarded, not by trying to help me, or even by asking me what was wrong. No, I was rewarded by being sent to the remedial class. I think they just thought I'd be better off out of the way of the 'normal' children. Many of the backward children had severe behaviour problems, too, and they probably thought I could cause less trouble if I was put in with all of them. But more than anything, I'm sure that I was sent to the remedial class purely as a kind of punishment.

CHAPTER THIRTEEN

There was no planning, no preparation, no time to go home and get used to the idea. I was to join the hut that very afternoon, immediately in fact. Mum went home and left me in the care of Mr Jackson. The first thing he did was to march me to my normal class to pick up my things to take to the hut. Any man with an ounce of humanity would have let me quietly collect my stuff or even go and collect my things himself, leaving without a word. But not Mr Jackson. My headmaster instead stood me in front of the class and, evil bastard that he was, instructed me to announce to all my classmates where I was going.

'So, tell your friends where you're going, Sophie,' he ordered.

'The hut,' I mumbled.

'The hut, yes,' he repeated like a parrot. 'And why are you going to the hut, Sophie? Tell everyone.'

'Because I was bad,' I whispered. My usual bravado was gone. My face was turned down to the floor, too ashamed to look at anyone.

'We can't hear her, can we, children?' the sadist went on. 'Say it louder!'

I started to cry again, in front of the whole class. I felt hot and sick and mortified with shame. And then the unthinkable happened.

I began, uncontrollably, to urinate. I didn't run to the loo. I just stood stock still, petrified with horror as warm urine trickled down my legs.

'Errrr! Miss! She's weeing!' one little boy shouted, and the whole class erupted in laughter, with screams of excited disgust and delight.

'Dirty girl!' shrieked Mrs Bray.

This woman had once made me a paper crown with gold stars to wear as a reward for being such a good pupil. But a little bit of urine was apparently sufficient for her to change her opinion of me entirely. Feeling almost unable to breathe, I began to hysterically cry-choke with mortification and horror.

'I don't know what you're crying about,' scolded Mrs Bray nastily. 'You're not the one who has to clear it up!'

They all hated me now, so I thought. I had no one left. Not a friend, not a teacher, not a parent who cared. Standing in that classroom of whooping children, disgraced, terrified and dripping in now-cold urine, I actually wanted to die.

But there was one kind soul in the midst of all these monstrous people. Mr Jackson and Mrs Bray called Mrs Crowley to take me away and change my wet things. Mrs Crowley was a woman who used to come in a few times a week to help with art and craft and who occasionally took a class herself. This was before the days of official 'teaching assistants' but I think that is how we would now describe her. All the children loved Mrs Crowley. She was a large woman, plump and maternal. She never shouted or scolded. She merely heaped praise on us, complimenting our crayon scrawlings and ugly lumps of clay, as if she were critiquing the work of artistic geniuses.

'Ah, Mrs Crowley,' said Mr Jackson pompously. 'Sophie has decided to wet herself. Could you take her to the girls' toilet and get her changed? Thanks so much.'

Mrs Crowley came in, took my hand in hers and led me out of the still-laughing room of former classmates. She took me, not to stand naked in the cold girls' toilet to clean up, but to a warm and quiet empty classroom with a sink. She washed me down with warm water, soap and a flannel and wrapped me in a towel, muttering comforting words constantly - *Poor baby, there you go, my lovely, Auntie Jackie make it better, it's all okay, my lovely.*

Usually when a child had an accident, they were made to change into clothes from the lost property bag, a stale-smelling collection of dirty and discarded rags. Auntie Jackie Crowley picked through the bag of lost property carefully, discarding most things and settling on a clean skirt and pair of tights to dress me in. They looked almost brand-new. As if sensing my revulsion at having to wear second-hand undergarments, she didn't give me any pants to wear, rejecting all the greying bits of underwear in the bag without even inspecting them.

'You don't want to wear someone else's dirty knickers, do you?' she said in a comedy voice. This made me laugh a little bit.

Before we left, she looked me in the eyes and held my little hands and said, 'And if anyone *ever* tries to hurt you again, you come and tell Auntie Jackie. Promise?'

I nodded and she gave me a big hug, holding me close against her huge, motherly bosom.

She must have known, or at least suspected. Back in the day before we were taught to recognise symptoms of abuse, this one woman had the sense to realise that when a child suddenly begins to act out, it almost certainly means something terrible has happened. A child who suddenly changes behaviour doesn't need punishment; she needs help. Of all the adults in my life at the time, only Mrs Crowley had the sense to know this. Perhaps she had been abused herself. Or perhaps her intuition was just way ahead of its time.

When I look back at my life, some people stand out like beacons of light. Jackie Crowley was one of them. I still consider her actions that day to be amongst the greatest and sweetest kindnesses ever bestowed on me. If only I could have thanked her properly. If only she could have known what her gentleness and humanity meant to me. If there is one person who I hope reads this book, one person who reads these words and recognises these events, it is her... dear Mrs Crowley.

CHAPTER FOURTEEN

And so I began my new school life in a remedial class of 'bad' children. The hut was less a classroom and more of a zoo, with the teacher, appropriately named Miss Grimm, spending most of the day engaged in little more than crowd control, doing her best to stop her charges from either killing her, themselves or each other. Looking back, I realise some of these 'backward' children were probably victims of abuse, too. Every day children would scream and moan and wet or defecate themselves. One boy, Jason Morrow, would frequently get his willy out to show the girls. He was abnormally sexual for such a little boy, often trying to grab the girls' crotches and triumphantly declaring, 'I got her fanny! I got my finger in her fanny!' Once I remember him turning around, shouting, 'Look!' His trousers were pulled down and his penis was out of his pants. It was sticking out straight, red and swollen. I thought it was the most disgusting thing I had ever seen. We were both only eight years old. When Jason's younger sister, Linda, joined the school she was like a little mad thing: a tiny explosive force of screaming, violently crazy behaviour. She would bite the teachers and other children or take her clothes off and wee straight onto the floor, laughing her head off. She didn't actually last long in mainstream school but was sent away to 'special school', so unruly was her behaviour. When we got to the age of eleven and went off to secondary schools, Jason also went on to 'special school' as it was then called. Wasn't it completely *obvious* that both children were being sexually abused?

I don't remember ever doing any actual schoolwork in the hut. I remember doing a lot of artwork and craft. I also remember being given laminated sheets with words spelled out in dots. We were to use a felt-tipped pen to join the dots and so learn to form our letters - hardly an educational task for a girl who was used to making and writing her own little books.

I had just one friend in the hut. Nicola Harding was a strange, wispy little girl but she was gentle, kind and quiet. Nicola seemed to spend most of her day intently staring around the room, as if she were an undercover agent, watching every little thing that happened. But I thought she was very, very clever. She had quite a posh voice and used really grown-up words. She could play the recorder better than anyone in the school and was always made to perform solos at the Christmas concerts and in assemblies while the parents and teachers looked on adoringly. But she really never did any work, not *any*. While we were scribbling on sugar paper with wax crayons, or penning 'the dog eats his dinner' in dots on a plastic page, Nicola would sit, and look…and look. She never lost her temper or shouted. When the other children were throwing tantrums, Nicola would grip my hand under the table in her sticky little fist and whisper, 'Keep very still. The bad boys are shouting. We must keep quiet 'til they stop.' We didn't speak much or play many games, being content to stand huddled together in a corner during break times. But Nicola was a huge comfort to me in my years in the hut.

Sometimes, on wonderful magical days, Mrs Crowley would come to the hut to do some painting or pottery work.

'How are my best darlings today?' she would ask as she entered the hut. She watched us all closely, smiling always, speaking with her calm, quiet voice. We all adored her. Even the most unruly children would sit still and smile when Mrs Crowley entered the room. She sometimes took me on her lap to draw, though I was a lump of a nine-year-old by now. She never mentioned that terrible day when I wet myself, never asked me any questions. But just having her around turned the day into Christmas. Even when I hadn't seen her for some weeks, I think perhaps the knowledge that Mrs Crowley was in school somewhere kept me sane.

It's fair to say that my behaviour did improve while I was in the hut. I simply couldn't compete for attention with the wildness of the other children (they often left me stunned and subdued into silence). I also cannot underestimate Nicola's calming influence. She was a charismatic and enigmatic child, and I grew to admire her greatly. I became quiet and withdrawn as she was. I didn't misbehave badly in front of Nicola – I would have felt disgraced, like I was letting her down. I remember Nicola as a sort of misunderstood genius. I like to think perhaps she is now doing wonderful things, saving the world or curing cancer. When we finally left the hut to join secondary schools, Nicola's family moved away. I never saw her again.

CHAPTER FIFTEEN

At home, Mum seemed relieved that my behaviour was going from out of control to merely withdrawn. But she became unreasonably intolerant, viewing any instance of bad behaviour as some sort of slight to her.

'I can't *cope* with your behaviour today, Sophie!' she would so often say, even for the slightest misdeed such as fidgeting or dropping my school bag on the floor, rather than hanging it up properly.

'Just go to your room and give us all some peace,' she would say at the drop of a hat.

My manners at mealtimes were expected to be exemplary, while my little brother and sister were allowed to waste food, throw things, drop cutlery on the floor and eat with their mouths open. Often I would be banished to eat meals in my room and, for the main part, I didn't mind this. I would lock myself away and lie on my bed, reading, writing stories, peeling the wallpaper from the walls in little bits, or unravelling the knots on the rug until it fell to pieces.

My older brother and sister rallied around my mother, taking every opportunity to tell on me. *Mum, come and see what Sophie's done. Mum, it's Sophie again. Mum, she won't behave!* My older brother, Michael, even took to blaming me for things I hadn't done. He would break something, steal something, or make one of the little ones cry and then announce that I had done it. He once even kicked a football through the living room window and ran to Mum to tell her I had broken it. And my mother believed him, gave me a slap, and sent me to my room, even though she'd never once seen me kick a football in my life. I took to playing only with my younger brother and sister, though they were only tiny. I was happy to play at dressing up as fairies with my little sister, Lisa, or exploring the garden with my little brother, Tom, even though I was really too old for those sorts of games. Spending time with the little ones was better than trying to play with the older children who I couldn't trust and who seemed to hate me. I also found friendship in my pets, particularly my cat, Mistletoe. She would play with boxes and bits of string or sit purring contentedly on my lap for hours at a time. The books of Enid Blyton, too, were an enormous comfort to me. I particularly loved the stories of the Famous Five though they were old-fashioned, racist and unacceptably misogynist by today's standards. I remember one of the boys praising Georgina, the tomboyish girl, with these very words: *'Well done! You're as good as a boy, any day'*. But despite the questionable undertones of these books, I found them absolutely thrilling. The idea that a group of children could go away and live alone in a hut or a secluded house was wonderful to me. I remember one where the four children and the dog went away and stayed on a deserted island, just by themselves but bringing a cow with them for milk. I was spellbound by this idea and spent my time planning adventures in remote places. It was probably the Famous Five that had inspired my desire to run away from home with Joanne.

In my mind I often replayed the events of that terrible weekend. But each time, I would change the ending. Sometimes I would run away from the tent and be picked up by a police car. Sometimes Martin's car would crash and I would be taken home in an ambulance. Very often I would fight Martin off and say all sorts of clever and intelligent things to stop him. These rehearsed conversations went on constantly in my head, and they often kept me awake at night.

I wasn't always unhappy but I was always accompanied by *That* lurking somewhere - on my shoulder, behind me, on the edge of my consciousness.

At some point after I was sent to the hut, I began to keep a sort of diary. I stole exercise books from school and filled them at night in my room with all sorts of ramblings. I wrote about other children mostly, who had done what that day and what they had said. I wrote about my mother and siblings and what I had been told off for that day. I wrote about the boys a lot. I hated boys, all boys. I thought they were dirty, wee-smelling, disgusting rat-like creatures. I even grew to hate my own brothers as they became older. I hated them for their breath and their farting and their greasy hair and their dirty penises. I wrote that I would never have a boyfriend and I would live alone on an island. I suppose these books were a kind of diary.

Thoughts of *That* were my constant, nagging companions but I never, ever wrote in my diaries about Martin or what happened in the tent. That was too horrible to write down, too horrible to think about intentionally and in detail. It was better to just leave it nagging at my awareness than lay it all out on paper, to set it all in stone, to make it even more real than it already was.

I kept these diaries hidden under the carpet at the edge of my room and to my knowledge, my mother never found them. But even if she had discovered my books, she probably would never have mentioned it. That was what she was like. She hated confrontation and messy feelings and generally would do anything for an easy life.

Sadly, only one of these books still survives and it has only a few pages written in it. But from what I can see, I was ahead of my years in literacy. Looking back, I feel writing in these books formed a large part of my education. I always was (and still am) appalling at maths, having had almost no real instruction past learning to count and do basic sums. But I think keeping these diaries must have kept my literacy levels up. I may have done nothing but dot-to-dots in school all day, but between reading Enid Blyton and writing my diaries, I started secondary school with a very acceptable grasp of reading and writing.

CHAPTER SIXTEEN

I mumbled and sulked and wasted my way through secondary school, sitting countless detentions and with frequent trips to the headmaster's office. But at least I was out of the remedial class now: my literacy levels were now far too high to warrant that. I came out with a few 'O' Levels - not great grades but enough for me to go to the local technical college to study for a couple of 'A' Levels.

My first boyfriend came along when I was sixteen. He didn't last long. I just wasn't interested in being remotely physical with him. I found kissing revolting and sex was out of the question. I wasn't terrified of men. I just found them disgusting. Even now it makes me feel a bit sick just to remember those spitty, tonguing teenage snogs and those sticky groping hands as they tried to get their hands inside my blouse. I hear a lot about girls who are abused becoming very promiscuous sexually and even ending up working as prostitutes. My experience was the complete opposite. Sex just didn't come into the picture. It was out of the question, as if it didn't apply to me somehow. I knew 'what people did' already and I wanted no part of it. And if sex is just 'what boys did' then I didn't want boys, simple as that.

I didn't have sex properly until I was twenty-six. I say 'properly' because this was always a contentious issue in my mind. I don't know to this day whether Martin actually had full sex with me. It really bothers me that I don't know when my 'first time' was. I know it shouldn't trouble me, but it does. I know he *probably* didn't have full sex with me. But perhaps he did. However, I can't just decide to believe something when I know very well it could be false.

I don't hate men any more, but even now sex doesn't interest me. I love to be affectionate, to cuddle and walk holding hands or arm in arm. I just have no real drive when it comes to sex. I don't know what *lust* feels like and I don't think I have ever had an orgasm. For a long time I considered that I might be a lesbian. This would certainly have made things simpler! But when given the opportunity I never really wanted to be physical with women either. I would love to have a relationship, a husband even, but so far no man has been able to cope with my complete disinterest in sex. I would like my own children and I think I'd make a good mother. But I don't know if it will ever happen now. Time is running out for me and motherhood.

CHAPTER SEVENTEEN

I don't intend to bore you with the story of my teenage years and early adulthood. I could fill the pages and waste some space with droning about failed relationships, bouts of depression, my suicide attempt and all the useless therapists I experienced. But what would be the point? I am an adult now and, as an adult, I must grow to deal with these things, take them on the chin, and stop blaming others for the way my life turned out. I write about my childhood in detail because I was just a tiny child. I was a victim. But I am a victim no longer, and I refuse to tell stories about my adult misfortunes just to gain some sympathy or attention. If you want to feel sorry for me, please feel sorry for my eight-year-old self. Feel sorry for the little girl I was and the summer that was broken. Feel sorry for my poor, misunderstood and mistreated classmates. But don't feel sorry for me as an angry, fucked-up adult. I have become hard, you see. I no longer want pity nor help. I must take control of my own life and be responsible for it.

This story does have an ending, though I wouldn't necessarily call it a happy one. And it ends in early adulthood.

CHAPTER EIGHTEEN

I was twenty-four when it happened. Around this age I had recovered from my recent suicide attempt. I had taken pills and drunk vodka, enough to put me in hospital but not enough to cause any serious or permanent damage. When I woke up, I realised I was glad to be alive, rather than disappointed. That event marked something of a pivotal point in my life, having decided, once and hopefully for all, that living was preferable to dying. I had drifted through my teens and early twenties, doing nothing in particular, with no adventure and no desire to look for one. Following my suicide attempt, I realised it was time to turn my life around, to grasp it fully with both hands and actually start living rather than just existing.

At that time I was living away from home in my own bedsit (I moved out of my mother's home at eighteen, as early as it was possible to do so). I was studying to retake some 'A' Levels so I could apply to study for a PGCE. My 'A' Level grades first time around had been pitiful and I needed at least a couple of 'E' grades this time in order to get a place at teacher training college. My dream was to become a special needs teacher, specialising in primary age children. To help me on my chosen career path, I had arranged a sort of informal work experience with Oaklands, a local special needs school. I had an interview with the headmistress, Mrs Kempton, where we discussed how things would work.

Mrs Kempton was kindly and seemed to care a great deal about the children under her charge, a sharp contrast to my own special needs experience. I thought how nice it would be to work at a school such as Oaklands where the headmistress had such an interest in her children's welfare. She explained that I was to help out one or another of the full-time teachers each day with whatever odd jobs might need doing. But otherwise I was there to attend, observe, talk to the children, and just get an idea of what the job entailed. I would do this for five consecutive days. I was really looking forward to it.

It was on the Monday that it happened. I turned up nice and early to start my first day's work experience. I was met by Mrs Kempton and led into the staff room to be introduced to the other teachers. When I entered, a man was standing with his back to me at a worktop against the wall. He was washing out a cup and had set a kettle boiling to make tea or coffee.

'Ah, Mr Brett,' said Mrs Kempton. 'This is Miss Jenkins. She's on work experience with us this week.' The man turned to face me and automatically held out his hand. He just smiled, shook my hand and returned to making his tea. I froze inside as I dropped his hand.

Oh, God! Is that HIM?

Mrs Kempton continued around the room, introducing me to various staff members. They must have thought me an odd sort of person as I barely spoke, I shook hands, I nodded but I asked no questions and entered into no friendly chit-chat. Perhaps they thought I was simply nervous, being not yet qualified and much younger than all of them. This was partly true. Nervous, I was, but not because of my age or lack of qualifications. I was nervous because I was almost certain that the man who had first shaken my hand, who was now sitting drinking his coffee and reading the paper, was none other than Martin, my abuser from sixteen years ago. But his name didn't ring any bells. Martin Brett? I thought his name was Bloom. We left the staff room and returned to Mrs Kempton's office to discuss things. My mind was boiling. I must have looked a little agitated because at one point she said, 'Are you feeling alright, Miss Jenkins?'

'I've just got a bit of a headache,' I lied. 'I didn't sleep very well last night.' This much was true; I still *never* slept well at night. The bed-wetting may have stopped, but the nightmares were still very frequent and I often lay awake until the small hours.

I struggled to regain my composure and force the thoughts of Martin from my mind. Somehow, I got through the day, busying myself with talking to children, losing myself in their concerns and needs. While at school I was in relative safety because it was easy to stay distracted, but all the time *That* was waiting somewhere at the back of my mind. For the rest of that day it felt as if a sort of looming beast was watching me, waiting until I was alone.

When I was at my most vulnerable it would strike.

School couldn't last forever. At four o'clock I was alone again, standing outside the school and waiting for a bus home. The moment I stepped onto the bus, the beast pounced, almost overwhelming me with waves of horror and emotion. I somehow bought my ticket and collapsed into a seat. Almost immediately I began to sob uncontrollably. I couldn't stop; I just couldn't contain the emotion. Huge proper tears were falling and my body was convulsing with sobs. People began to fidget at the embarrassment of watching a grown woman weep out loud in public, but they didn't move. Only one elderly woman sitting across the aisle leaned in and asked, 'Are you alright, dear?' I nodded. She seemed content with my answer, as did the rest of the bus, probably relieved that someone had asked the socially necessary question, 'Are you alright?' Then she, and they, returned to their thoughts and ignored me for the rest of the journey. I arrived at my stop, walked the short distance home, and put the key in the door to my bedsit.

It was a very strange night. I cried for a full three or four hours. I ate nothing, I drank nothing, and the really bizarre thing was that I *thought* nothing. You are probably expecting me to tell you that my mind was full of visions of that night, or of what to do next, or of revenge, or of whether I should tell the headmistress or the police, and so forth. But it was as if I had lost all power of thought. My mind seemed so intent on crying that it had no energy left for thinking. When people say 'my mind went blank' that isn't just a dramatic thing to say; sometimes it's really true. I know because I have experienced it.

I cried until my throat was sore and my eyes were stinging and bloodshot. When I caught sight of myself in the mirror I saw that my face was red and blotchy and I looked like I had some terrible disease from mediaeval times, some sort of plague or pox.

I don't know when I stopped crying, but at some point I know I fell into a deep sleep on the sofa – something very unusual for me. I remember waking many hours later, when it was dark; perhaps it was three or four in the morning. I was terribly dehydrated, my throat parched, and I was desperate for a drink. I started to move but immediately I sensed something wasn't right. My clothes were damp with sweat. That wasn't like me at all, especially as it was so cold.

And then I realised the dampness wasn't sweat: I had wet the bed.

CHAPTER NINETEEN

I managed to get into Oaklands the next day but only by convincing myself that I could have been mistaken about that man actually being Martin. It was quite possible that he was a completely innocent and pleasant man, I told myself. I had had only a glimpse of his face and hadn't heard him speak at all. Probably, I reasoned, Mr Brett simply had a similar look to my abuser and my mind had filled in the blanks. After all, it was *sixteen years ago*. Heartened by these thoughts, I turned up for my second day at Oaklands. Even so, my heart was pounding as I entered the staff room that morning. But I needn't have worried because Mr Brett didn't seem to be there. I was free to go about my day, sitting in on a class of very young children, helping them form their letters, and reading to them.

I didn't see him again until almost the end of the day, when I was asked to sit in on a meeting of some sort. When I entered the room, everyone else was already sitting and Mr Brett had his back to me. I sat to the side of him, a little way away, and could get a clear look at his face. I stared at him as Mrs Kempton spoke, talking about some administrative issue or other. *I still wasn't sure.* It looked a lot like Martin. I would like to say his image had been etched indelibly into my mind for all eternity, but it *hadn't.* My memory was a bit fuzzy in this regard. Could I be wrong about this kindly special needs teacher being a filthy sexual pervert, a paedophile, the worst kind of human being put on this earth?

But then he spoke.

'I think the point we all have to remember is....'

I don't remember what else he said. If my memory of his face was hazy, my memory of his voice certainly wasn't. It was him, speaking with that familiar, gravelly smoker's voice and revealing those stick-like teeth.

My heart leapt and I sharply and audibly drew in my breath. He looked straight at me, surprised at my sudden gasp, showing no sign of recognising the child he had attacked sixteen years before.

I looked him up at down. *The fingers, what about the yellow fingers?* I looked to his hands, and to my sinking horror I could see the same brownish yellow stains, fainter than before but still definitely visible.

He had cleaned himself up a lot. His teeth were no longer yellow and he had worked to scrub the nicotine stains from his fingers. He obviously looked older, perhaps even thinner, almost gaunt and much greyer. His face was deeply lined and he looked closer to sixty, though he was probably only around forty-five. But it was him. Him, him, *him*! My childhood abuser was sitting just two chairs away from me; a paedophile, working in a school full of the most vulnerable children in society.

I felt strangely calm. Partly I think this was because the room full of people seemed to offer some security. But also, the night's outpouring of emotion had simply drained me so completely. I had nothing left.

He clearly noticed as I continued to stare at him because he began surreptitiously glancing back at me, shifting uneasily in his chair and fidgeting more than was necessary – clearing his throat, clicking his pen, turning his pages to look at non-existent notes. That actually pleased me a little. I was making him feel uncomfortable and I felt a little braver.

I don't know where it came from, but out of nowhere I heard myself asking, 'Do I know you from somewhere?' Perhaps it was the relative safety of that room full of adults, perhaps it was the empowerment of knowing I had already unsettled him, but somewhere I had found the courage to confront him. To this day, I am still proud of myself for that moment of bravery.

'No, I don't think so,' he replied, not looking back at me but becoming ridiculously flustered.

When I look back now, I still am not sure that he had recognised me at this point. What I do think is likely is that he suspected me of being *one* of his victims and that he was frantically trying to work out which one. I have no doubt that I was only one of many child victims of Martin Brett. Perhaps his other victims had special needs or were carefully chosen to be those who would be least likely to be believed. I'm sure he didn't expect to be confronted, off-guard, by one of them in his place of work, surrounded by trusted colleagues.

'Are you okay, Martin?' asked one of the others.

'Yeah, yeah… I just… forgot something,' he mumbled and then picked up his papers and walked out of the room.

I was flabbergasted. Here he was, the thing of nightmares, the monster under my bed, the bogeyman who had haunted my nights and days for sixteen years, brought low, mumbling, stumbling and forgetting his words.

He was afraid of *me!*

I want to address all those of you who are adults now but have been victims of child abuse yourselves. I know there will be many of you reading this book, wondering what would happen if you ever came across your abuser again.

I can't tell you how that would go. I can't advise you to confront him, threaten him, or try to overpower him. But I can say this: When you're an adult, *they just aren't so scary any more*. Whoever abused you, and however terrified you were at the time, there is no need to be afraid any more. He cannot hurt you again. He does not have power over you simply by virtue of being an adult to your tiny child. You and he are now equals.

That is how I saw it when I finally met Martin again after all those years.

In the days that followed the meeting, I tracked him down, following him around school whenever I could, watching him as he squirmed to avoid my gaze. I took a sort of sick pleasure in making him feel uncomfortable.

I asked Mrs Kempton if I could sit in on his class, which included several children with Down syndrome. I wasn't very experienced with this sort of problem, I told Mrs Kempton, and I would love to spend some time with these children. So I spent the final three days of my work experience watching him while he worked. To the children I was all smiles, but whenever I looked his way my face was stony and mean. Only sometimes would I let a small, sneering smile creep over my face as I looked at him, judging him, unsettling him. He barely spoke to me in three days, and never once looked me in the eye.

Bullied had become the bully. Victim had become the tormentor. I spent those three days making Martin Brett feel as uncomfortable as I possibly could, making him feel the teeniest taste of what he had made me feel. I almost began to enjoy myself. I had somehow turned it around. I now had the power. He couldn't hurt me any more. He could never hurt me again.

But I could hurt him! I could bring him down, disgrace him, or have him arrested. I could make him lose his job, his friends: I could change his life beyond all recognition.

But don't get me wrong: I was not without fear during these days. I barely slept and my mind was constantly whirring with thoughts of what I would do next or what I would or wouldn't say to him. I made up long conversations in my head, detailing the exact things I would say, his responses and my clever replies. But when I was in the same room as him, generally I said very little. In fact, we only ever had one more conversation and, unbelievably, it was in front of just the children. In public places like this, I felt somehow safer and brave enough to confront him. I said only sixteen words. One for each year I had lived since the event. Those sixteen words sealed his fate. *Remember the dog you gave me? I kept it. It is still covered in your DNA.*

CHAPTER TWENTY

Perhaps you are expecting this story to end in an exciting climax of revenge, a huge dramatic finale where he is thrown in prison, or whereby I get hold of a gun and shoot him. I'm sorry to disappoint you but the truth is much more mundane.

I never did tell the police. I never told anyone else. And I never said another word to Martin Brett.

It must have been a couple of months later: I was walking past a newsagent when the headline on a local newspaper caught my eye. I picked up a copy and read the front-page story. A local special needs teacher had hanged himself from a tree. He left no wife, no children. He had been a bit of a loner, so the paper said, but had been well liked in the school where he worked.

Money troubles were suspected as the reason for his suicide.

My first feelings on reading the news were odd. I wish I could tell you I felt instant relief but this is not how it happened. Briefly, I felt a kind of guilt - not because I had almost certainly had some sort of effect on his decision to kill himself, because I felt nothing in that regard. The slight guilt I felt was more a feeling that someone might find out, somehow someone might know that I had pushed a man to suicide. For a couple of weeks I was waiting for a knock at the door from the police, investigating his suspicious death, asking what I knew about it. In our small village, a story like this was big news and the papers ran it for some time.

More details were released each day. Apparently the noose he had tied hadn't tightened properly around his neck and he had taken a long time to die. That seemed appropriate somehow and I felt no pity.

As the weeks passed the story disappeared from the papers and the world forgot about Martin Brett. Bizarrely, I felt disappointed. This had all been such a huge anti-climax and I couldn't quite believe it was all over so suddenly. *What's next?* I kept thinking. *There has to be more.*

It was a very gradual process that I noticed only really in hindsight. But in the months that followed, the feelings of disappointment and guilt ebbed away. In their place came feelings of peace, calmness and even a sort of contentment. The greatest miracle of all was that I began to sleep, deeply, through the night. Sometimes the old nightmares would return (sometimes they still do): I would be naked and looking for a toilet. But in the main, my dreams became sweeter, and just full of the normal nonsensical rubbish of which everyone else dreams.

Around this time I began to write things down. First of all it was just brief notes, thoughts or memories. But then came the day when I just sat down and started at the beginning, writing down the whole story in every tiny detail. I think on the first day I wrote three thousand words. As the thoughts began to flow, the story just fell out of me. There was very little effort. It was almost as if it had been waiting all this time to be told. But I did nothing with it. It was not for publication. It was just for me.

Then I met Kate Skylark. She had published books before and was presently ghost-writing a child abuse story, longer and more terrible than mine. I eventually plucked up the courage to let her read my own story. I sat in her living room while she read, watching her wipe away tears. With a bit of polishing, she told me, this story was well worth publishing, and she would be happy to help me get it into shape for release as a book.

I didn't hesitate. I realised instantly that I *wanted* my story to be out there. I wanted others to know how brave I had been in the presence of my attacker. I was *proud* of myself. I wanted people to know about that, even if only anonymously. And so Kate I worked together to turn *Dirty Little Dog* into a publishable book. I told the story, in more detail than I had ever done before. We both cried a lot but it was a wonderful experience.

But I was adamant about one thing. I insisted that a proportion of any profits raised from sales of this book had to go to children's charities. This condition was essential for my peace of mind. That way, I knew that writing this book would not just help me, but that it would help other children. It might even help to stop children from being abused. And if writing this book could stop even *one* child from being abused, then it would be a thousand times worth it.

So that was my story. That was the story of how a dirty little toy dog was responsible for erasing Martin Brett, paedophile and child abuser, from my life. The little dirty dog put a stop to a story that might have gone on for my entire life. I'm not one hundred per cent 'over it'. But it *is* over. All that's left is for me to forgive my mother.

I'm working on that.

Thanks for reading my story. I hope it was a positive experience for you. Please remember, for every book sold or borrowed, Kate and I will make a donation to the NSPCC. So just by downloading this little book you may have helped a child to stay safe.

Thanks so much for reading,

Sophie.

****

If you enjoyed this book, please check out

Daddy's Wicked Parties

Another shocking childhood memoir by
Kate Skylark *with Lucy Gilbert*

Steve Gilbert is a charming, clever man. Lucy is his ten-year-old daughter. Lucy loves him to bits, just as all little girls love their daddies and she is delighted to hear he has organised a special party for her. After all, little girls love parties. But Steve Gilbert is also a sociopathic, manipulative sexual predator. Brainwashed into accepting her father's twisted view of the world, Lucy trusts him implicitly. Daddy will keep her safe; he will keep her happy. Daddy would never betray his little girl, would he? But as time goes on, Steve Gilbert's evil manipulations escalate and following a shocking string of events, Lucy's innocent young life turns from simple happy childhood to an abusive nightmare.

Only one person can save her now.